LIGHT IN THE DARKNESS

# NORAH KATE

## TO HAVE NEVER HELD YOU

**ryan baker**

2020

Black Coral Press

**Dedicated to my wife**
And to those who have suffered or are suffering the loss of a child

# Table of Contents

# Bright Days, Dark Nights

We were blessed with a boy, my Light Giver, in November of 2012. He was a lively little one. Fearless and curious. He loved water—baths, swimming pools, oceans, anything he could get himself into—to the endless fear and worry of his mother and me. His bright, chocolaty eyes. His wind-tossed brown hair. He wasn't a colossus (like our now third born) but he was big. He was rough and tumble.

Then on May 3, 2014, just a year and a half later, my wife told me amazing and life-altering news: we were pregnant again!

## Woot! Woot!

I was elated. I couldn't wait. I looked forward to a new baby; which is odd, because I'm not a baby person, not even a little kid person.

All my life I'd spent trying to avoid the smaller humans that shared this planet with me. As a matter of fact, I had done such an incredible job that I had avoided ever even holding a baby until a month or so before my Light Giver was born. My wife shoved her best friend's daughter into my arms. It was hold or drop.

Don't worry, I held.

Awkwardly. Really awkward at first.

Even with my first born, holding a baby didn't change. It was still awkward, but something in me changed. I was head-over-heels for this kid. I fell in love with my baby. I'm still not a "kid person,m" but man I love getting down and playing with my boys. My kids don't have to play by the same rules as everyone else's—I am all about them.

So, back to May 3, 2014. The joy I had in my heart couldn't be held in. I was at a soul-crushing job, but my soul was happy. My days were spent wondering if it was going to be a boy or a girl. I wondered how my Light Giver would handle having us divide our time between him and our new baby. Would he love this new addition or loathe the attention he or she got?

We had time to work on him and make sure he was just as excited as us. He was only a year-and-a-half; but man, we were going to make this fun.

Everything was ticking along just fine. We were scouring books and the interwebs for names. The meaning of the name is of great importance to both my wife and me. We believe that, while it doesn't dictate your life, the meaning of your name has a subconscious effect on your life. That is why I call my first born my Light Giver because that is what his name means—Giver of Light. We'd find names and write them down then share them and get the other's reaction. Some got crossed off immediately. Others got to hang around.

We weren't buying anything yet because we didn't know if it was a boy or girl. We also hadn't told many people (only our immediate family) because it was before twelve weeks. My wife being a nurse is quite the smart lady. With each of our kids, we waited to tell people we were pregnant until after the twelfth week because miscarriages were less likely after that point.

So we celebrated with the few that knew. They asked loads of questions but always checked in on my wife to make sure she was doing well and to see if she needed anything.

I mean, life was pretty amazing.

But life has a way of taking you down paths you wouldn't go yourself. It has a way of darkening the sun, of bringing a drowning rain, and leaving you empty. And it did to us. It was a horrible moment. The moment when you go to the doctor for a routine checkup...

*And there's no heartbeat.*

# Insufficient

To say that sorrow and grief were too tame of words is an understatement. Misery. Desolation. Despondent. Hopeless. Those words do a bit better a job of describing the hollowness that was pervasive. There were some days that our Light Giver was the only reason we moved. Without him, I don't know what we would have done.

He didn't know the weight we felt. He didn't understand fully what we meant when we said we were pregnant. His smile didn't fade. His joy didn't lapse. His cheer, his life, his *light* didn't flicker. It didn't dim. It shone brightly. Though the rot was in our bones, we found a way to smile. The cute ways he spoke. His intrepid attitude. It kept us on our toes, it kept us moving, it got us out of bed in the morning, and it made us smile during the day.

We were thankful we hadn't told people. It was going to be sickening telling the few that knew. But we did. And it was a good thing.

Now we had a small support group around us. Our mothers could jump in and be with my wife in this time unlike I could. I did everything I could to mourn with her, be with her, and help bring a smile to her face. But I will never know the joys and the pains of actually carrying a baby.

I simply cannot relate. I can try and empathize to the best of my abilities. But those who have borne children can relate on a deeper level that I simply cannot.

*She should have been born on January 8, 2015.*

Instead, we were left with a hole in our hearts. A void. An abyss that sucked me in hard. It felt like a black hole. We had danced too close and found ourselves being drawn into the darkness against our wills.

We hurled our sadness and pain, our grief and sorrow, our loss and anger at God. I figure, if He's big enough to create us, He's big enough to deal with me. Pissed off, angry, and bitter. I was so desperate, so discouraged, so hopeless during the first couple of months. At the time I was a teller at a bank, and numerous times I had to excuse myself to go get some water. I had to replenish what was draining out of my eyes so violently.

Ok, so I wasn't blubbering at work; but it was a difficult task to hold back my tears.

The days seemed long. Our Light Giver gave us joy. We cherished his life unlike we ever had. We were radically blessed with a healthy baby already. I'm sure we smothered him in hugs, and he had no idea why. The simple act of cuddling up with him was cathartic.

Then one day I remember telling my wife that I thought it would be really good for us to pray and ask God to tell us if it had been a boy or a girl. That in knowing we could find a name and stop calling this child an "it." Because "it" was a child of God, so dearly loved that He had called this child to His side before we ever put our arms around it.

# To Have Never Held You

That still hurts at times. Knowing that I will never hold my second child in this life. Knowing I'll never get to see what color eyes she had, what color hair. To never have her tiny hands grip my finger. To see her toothless grin. To hear her laugh. I'll never get to cuddle her in my arms, sing her a bedtime song, pray with her.

*It still hurts.*

So we prayed. And prayed. And, well, we prayed a little more to make sure. I sheepishly dodged the question for a bit. I wanted to know, but I also was scared I'd think I heard one thing and she'd think the other. My wife came up to me and brought it about: *what did you hear?*

Whoa. This is about to be real.

I looked her in the eyes. Searching them, hoping I'd somehow see into her mind and see what I had heard from God. But I didn't. So I mustered up my courage…

"A girl." I smiled.

She smiled, too.

And I knew then, before any words came out, that I hadn't made it up in my mind. That what she heard was in agreement with what I did. That God had given us a girl.

*The entire event shifted; instead of having a wound, we had a daughter.*

So we went back to the drawing board for names. It didn't take too long for us to agree. Our precious Norah Kate—our Light (Norah) of Purity (Kate) or Pure Light. I like Pure Light because light cannot be held. Also, it can't be overpowered by darkness.

That's one of the most beautiful aspects of light. No matter how dark you make a room, turn on one little light, spark one small candle, and there is light. There is a glow. It is distinctive and open. Now, the darkness is being overcome by light. You cannot turn on darkness or pile enough up on top of the light to put it out.

Darkness is overcome by light.

# Words

Eventually, I began opening up about it from time to time. It had only been a couple months, but talking with close friends brought it out. It was met with disbelief.

I want to be genuine here while not being rude to some people. If you have experienced a miscarriage, finding others who have is a good thing. Friends who haven't experienced a miscarriage don't quite understand. I was given some "encouragement" that felt more like a backhanded slap than love. Now, the men I talked to at the time were trying to be real, trying to be uplifting, trying to be encouraging to me. There was no ill-will within them when they spoke to me.

But sometimes, they didn't say the right thing. Sometimes, actually, they flat out said the wrong thing. And it hurt badly.

It's insult to injury, really. Being kicked while I was down. I ended up just closing my mouth and letting the subject mold and bend into something entirely new and different. I knew at the time they spoke it that they weren't trying to be insensitive or malicious. They were trying to brighten my spirits. They were. I realized that they may not be the best to talk with about this. That's all.

If you are going through a miscarriage, and it is the days, weeks, or months after, you may have some well-meaning people say some very hurtful words to you. There are a lot of respectable ways to handle it, and a lot of poor ways to handle it. I can't tell you how to handle each situation, but try to remember that they mean well. Try to turn the pain into love. Try to find your Pure Light that will one day make you smile, that diminishes the darkness.

If you are a friend of people going through a miscarriage, do us a favor. Either keep quiet and lend your *actions* rather than your words, or pray for us and with us. Speak life into us. Speak of God. Don't speak of how it could be worse, how others have suffered more. This will either get you yelled at or shut out. Validate their feelings, no matter what they are.

And listen.

This isn't a problem you can fix. There are no words you can speak, no actions you can do, that will change how things are right now. So shut up and listen. Girls, hug. Guys, bro hug. Unless the grieving parents are adamant about it, get them out of the house. Allow the pain to work its way out of them, but also, let them know that life can move on. Invite them to dinner, or take them dinner and chat it up.

Sometimes, not talking about it is the right way to go. Just be a friend. Use your words for building up.

# Years Removed

Every January I think of her. (Lets be real, I think of her every single day.) I think of the girl I never got to hold. I think of the girl that God saw fit to bring to His side before she ever experienced life here on Earth. I think about the Pure Light she has brought to us. Occasionally, I still feel the pangs of sorrow; but overall, when I think of my Norah, I smile.

Years have past since then. Something important I want to point out is this: *time did not heal this wound.* Time cannot heal. Time gives us the *opportunity* to heal. If we do nothing, if we wallow and seclude ourselves, we will not heal. But if we use the opportunity given to us to seek God, seek community, seek peace and healing, we will find it.

And with any major trauma, there will be scars. But these scars aren't hideous or left to remind us of our pain.

The scars we gather are our stories.

Our scares are what we can now use to give peace and grace and love and joy to those who have suffered in similar ways.

And my prayer is that this little book will do just that for you, that it will help the healing process. If it is recent, as in, there isn't a scar but an open gash bleeding out, scream and cry to God. Scream and cry with someone else. Literally scream. Literally cry. Men, that means you too. This whole book is written by me, a man. And if you want to doubt how "manly" I am, my job description is running into burning buildings.

**—So Men...**

Let me speak to any men reading this. I wouldn't be surprised if your wife told you to read it and you are doing it to please her, not because you would have sought this out. First, thanks for reading. Second, I don't believe in a lot of the junk going on that feels more like we are feminizing men than building them into adventure-seeking, rough-around-the-edges men who are genuine, self-aware, and defenders of our families. I feel a lot of our culture is shifting to emasculating men rather than building men into fortresses of refuge and grace. We are meant to be wild. We are meant to be rough and uncouth at times. We were meant for the mountains not the lattes.

So I'm not telling you to become a ball of emotions and have a tea party with your three closest buddies (pass the Earl Gray please). But I am telling you that running from emotions creates a wall that your wife, kids, family, and friends will not be able to relate. You'll be so stoic that the stoics will walk away.

That's stupid.

But you know what's not? Loading up the weights at the gym with a buddy or two and telling them that right now, life sucks. Lift some. Tell them that you and your wife had a miscarriage and that you want to ram your fist through the nearest wall. Lift some more. Get that anger out. Scream and yell at the gym. Sure, you'll be "that guy," but that won't last. Then people will forget you yelled and all will be normal.

And you'll have gotten some of it off your chest. While lifting. Or watching football. Or climbing a mountain using only one leg. I don't care—just do something with other guys and talk for five minutes. We usually don't need much more. Then, the next day, talk for five more minutes. Eventually, you might have talked about it for one whole hour and you'll feel like a new you.

You won't have blubbered or ugly cried. (Do guys ugly cry? Is that a thing?) But you'll have dealt with it in a super manly way that no one will discredit, and other men will actually realize they can talk to you in five minute increments and feel awesome themselves.

# Hidden in Darkness

Having been through a miscarriage now, I can tell you that it's not talked about a lot. I mean, sure, the internet will have medical and scientific journals on it. You'll find some blogs about it, maybe even some books. But really, this isn't talked about, not until someone experiences it and the devastation it brings. It's a human phenomenon that brings people together during pain, like it was programmed in us to reach out to the hurting during disaster.

Because so few people talk about miscarriages, lots of parents (including those who have had a miscarriage) are left in the dark. They are sent out to wonder if what is happening is normal or okay. It's like being on a skiff in the middle of a body of water at night. There's nothing out there to guide you, nothing to give you a direction or comfort that the pain will end.

And that sucks.

In one of the worst moments in a person's life, they are left alone. Well, it feels like that at least. Family and friends will be there for you, but so much of this is internal that it often feels like we are alone. However, there are so many people who have gone through this pain, who have found the edge of the darkness and come back into the light.

## Miscarriage is darkness.

What else could it be? What should have been one of the most intimate and beautiful experience in human life morphs into one of the most desperate, dark, and desolate times. What could have been different? What could we have done to save this child? Why did this happen? Why us? What...? Why...? What...? Why...?

Questions abound. Answers don't come.

That's partly because no one talks about it, partly because it's such an intimate and personal experience, and partly because there isn't much information out there for those who are suffering through it.

# Where do we go from here?

You're stranded on a boat in the middle of water in the darkness. What do you do? What *can* you do? There is a void within your chest. So in these moments of emptiness and pain, how do you dig yourself out? How do you get past this?

# You paddle.

And you paddle like hell is coming, because if you stay stagnant, hell will swallow you. Because it is. When you are in the middle of nowhere, it's not about finding a direction, it's about movement. With no bearing and no map, that movement starts with God. I've told you what I did. I physically screamed. I yelled. I yelled directly at God. I didn't hate him. I didn't hurl verbal abuse. I hurled my anger. I screamed out my pain. I asked why. I asked how could it be. I told Him it was a terrible thing to do. And in those moments, I didn't hear God. There wasn't a response as I'd imagined there would be.

There was no scolding, no how-dare-you-talk-to-me-that-way drivel. There was no anger from God. There was no hurt feelings or appalled behaviour. It wasn't like anything I expected. I expected a just response (or more clearly, "just" in the sense *I believed* it should be), or even silence. So what I felt next was startling.

A hug.

A blanket of love.

In those raw moments there was a sense of pride from God that I had come to Him. There was a pain and sadness that could only come from someone who has experienced loss in such a similar way. There was an embrace that told me, "give me everything—all this rage, all this pain, all this weight—and I will give you peace. I will give you grace. I will give you rest."

And I wept.

And I felt a peace brewing. I wasn't there yet. I wasn't at peace, but I was paddling to it. I was rowing. And I was rowing with all my might. I didn't have a guide or a direction; I had my arms and I was rowing.

Your first place should be at God's feet. Maybe you skipped that step. No harm done. Go back to him. (You don't even need to apologize. He's pretty cool.) You can do it alone. I don't believe my wife ever knew I would scream and yell, probably because most of the time it was in the car while driving home from work. I usually only felt comfortable doing it when I was alone. I'd scream at the top of my lungs. And a lot of times, it wasn't words. It was a good, old-fashioned ball of rage freeing itself from my heart.

After your authentic self encounters God, your rowing may take you to someone. There are two funny things that happen here. First, we don't often think a "someone" is God's answer. The other funny thing is, it might not be a "someone" you expect. I'm absolutely guilty of this. I think God's answer should be a change in my circumstance, not an addition into the mix of things. Raise your hand if that's what you think should happen when you pray for God's help.

You see, God is invisible. (See what I did there?)

But *we* are visible. We are physical. We have mass and density. And sometimes God brings along another physical being that has mass and density to be with us. And we keep waving at God saying, "Hey! What are you going to do about this?"

We want out. We want to hit the eject button, the "stop-this-crap" button. We want to push the "I'm-tired-of-this button" and magically be transported to a time when there isn't this pain, whether it's before or after the circumstance. So this new mass and density that has come into our lives sure can't be the answer to our prayers.

So I yelled some more at God, "I asked you to help me, to heal this wound, to help get me through this."

And I just see Him shaking His head with his hand over his face. He takes his hand away, smiles at me, and says, "you just don't get it. That mass and density *is* the answer to your prayer, because I'm not about teleportation, I'm about wading through the muck and the suck."

And looking at it from this side, from being on the land and not still in the boat rowing like a crazed lunatic that just found his freedom illegally, I see that *living* in the moment is exactly where God wants me. It's not because he's sadistic and cruel (it may *feel* that way), but because I'm learning and growing and turning more into who He wants me to be.

Life isn't about all the different ends that we will see but all the different journeys we will take and the stories we will be able to share.

# The End, The Journey

Life has never been about the various ends and destinations. It's not about the completion of one event and on to the next. Life is about living— living in the joy and love and elation of being pregnant. It's also about living in the horror and sorrow and desperation of losing a child.

It makes more and more sense the older I get, that the pain I suffer isn't always because of me (don't get me wrong, I have personally been the bearer of my own pain), but maybe I experience certain pains *for* someone else. Hopefully this book can be the beginning of your healing. Maybe one day I'll be the mass and density that God brings along in someone's life. I'll be able to use my experience to minister to someone else. Maybe God will use our shared pain to bring them to Himself.

I mean, think of that and how amazing that would be. God strategically allows me (you) to be in a horrible situation so that one day I (you) will be someone else's *answer to prayer*. When we start seeing that God created us in and for community, it makes a whole lot more sense that an answer to our prayer is a physical person rather than a sudden (i.e. magical?) change in circumstances that whisks away all the pain and suffering we might have had to go through.

## God, family, community, and yelling. Lots and lots of yelling.

That was my path. Your path may be different. That's okay. What isn't okay is sitting still in the water. Sometimes you just can't row. That's okay. There were some days I didn't row. There were some days that my motto for the day was "keep my Light Giver alive." And that was it. He's still alive and healthy. So even though I didn't row that day, I accomplished something.

Life doesn't stop because we are in pain. Life doesn't stop because ours wants to. The job still calls. Family and friends still call. Bills still come in the mail (yeah, those definitely don't stop). Appliances and electronics still break. *Life* still goes on. And I think that is good. It sucks for a moment, but putting one foot in front of the other has served me well. The cliche "when walking through hell, keep walking" applies. It's cliche because it works.

May you be able to tell your story one day. I pray no one would ever experience this pain; but until we are in our new bodies, we know it will happen again. So may you become the answer to another's prayers. May your scar be healing to another. May you paddle harder while you are in the darkness of miscarriage.

You are not flawed, but you are not enough either. God didn't design anyone to be enough. He designed us to be enough with Him and with each other. You are in a terrible season. What you feel is real and okay, whether you feel the most intense emotions you've ever felt in your life or absolutely nothing at all. Whether you are overwhelmed with sorrow or anger or bitterness or any other emotion, it is okay. Those emotions were designed to bring you to God. And God designed people to bring to you.

Keep paddling. Your imperfections are being perfected. Your light may be dim right now, but your fire will burn once more. Then hold on as God uses your new strength to absolutely wreck the darkness around others so His light will flood in.

# Him

As I said, I don't get to hold her. I don't get to see her, kiss her, and love her. I don't get to hear her little cries or her laughter. I don't get to see her smile. I don't get to hold her close when she gets hurt. I don't get to comfort her or smile with her.

That's a lot of don'ts and a lot of pain. And this is just one more reason why the ends never justify the means. What could this end possibly justify? The death of an innocent child could never be construed as good. But when we allow God to wash over us in these times, when we recognize that we will in fact have moments that we drown, we must understand that we have a God that is walking just above the sea that will reach down and pick us up, he will not only always be there, but that he will rebuke the waves and calm the sea for us.

We need only look to Him. We need only to focus on Him.

I believe that she is being held by her Father. She is warm. She is healthy. She is smiling. And most importantly, she isn't in pain. She wasn't marred by the imperfectness of this world. She'll never know pain—and I can rejoice in that. My Norah Kate will only know the love our Father gives. She will only have ever walked the streets of Heaven, rested in the arms of Grace, and found the purest of Joys.

God didn't give Norah Kate to me and my wife to be vicious. He didn't give her to us to hurt us and laugh. No, God doesn't give and take at whim. Her life gave my wife and me joy.

Her departure brought us to our knees.

Together.

And that is the point of pain—to draw us into Him and draw us together.

Miscarriages are terrible, and they are compounded by the fact that you feel so ashamed and so low that you don't want to share it with others. You want to, but you don't. So we did what most people do: we stayed silent. We spoke to very few people. What would people think if they knew we couldn't even make a kid properly?

How stupid these lies are that we believe! How ridiculous do we have to be to listen to the words of the Devil over the words of our Father? But yet we do again and again. We say horrible things to ourselves and then we don't talk about it in fear people will. . .do what? It's simply ludicrous to believe that people wouldn't rally around us.

We aren't strong enough, and we weren't even built to be able to handle it. Pain is our ultimate reminder that we were created less than capable. When we experience pain, we should automatically go to Him. It should be our call to run home to our Father. We are all marred. We are all marked. Some wounds are deep, some shallow. But we race to Him, and He will bring us a miracle of mass and density. He will bring us people who will experience life with us, drag us when we need to be dragged, jump with us when we are joyful, and talk when we are in need of wisdom.

# The Stories We Share

We all have stories that inspire us, even ones that don't have the outcome the protagonist wanted. Think of the stories of Olympians who fall during a race only to have another competitor come back and help them cross the finish line, or maybe a dad battle his way through security to lift up his son and cross the finish line. We see and hear those stories and not one person is thinking about the end.

They are thinking about the journey. They are thinking about the sacrifices made and the determination and will of the people to stand up and continue.

Yes, there is a finish line. Every race, every season, every circumstance has a finish. One thing ends and another begins. We all know that. Those aren't the parts we are inspired by. It's the rising up under pain, under adversity, under shame and forging ahead.

Life is about those stories. And when we stand up after the loss of a child, it is no less remarkable. This wound you now carry will leave a scar. But that scar reminds us that there is a faithful God and that we lived through it. I have that scar. My wife has that scar.

I'm not going to say it's a beautiful scar. I wish I didn't have it; I wish my wife didn't have it. But what is beautiful is becoming a light to someone else. What is beautiful is becoming home for another couple. What is beautiful is speaking out about it and knowing that my past can now be apart of your healing.

But in the mix of it, in the mire and muck, you aren't thinking about how one day this could be a story to share. You're thinking about your lost child. You're thinking about the sanctity of life, of a love lost.

And it's hell.

Know that you are being prayed for. I'm sure I don't know your name. I will probably never meet you. But I pray, even as I write this, for each and every person, couple, and family going through this. Cry out to God. Scream out to him. Have people over. Talk about it. What you feel is OK—anger, rage, sadness, sorrow, spite. At other times, have people over and don't talk about it. It will be in your head at all times, but it doesn't have to be all that you do.

There is a time to talk and there is a time to. . .not talk about it. Don't feel bad if you think, "I'm going to go out tonight with some friends." Husbands, let your wife free for a night of life-sustaining girlfriend fun. Wives, let your husband cater to that primitive side that denies all emotions and eats obscene amounts of pizza and donuts with other primitive friends.

And be together as a couple with friends. Go on a double or triple date. Enjoy a beautiful sandwich in a park or a fine dining experience at a high end restaurant, or anything in between; but do it together. Have moments with girl friends, have moments with guy friends, and have moments with couple friends.

Talk. And don't talk.

Both are life-giving. Both have their place.

These moments build us up. They are crafting our healing behind the scenes. We often think that these light-hearted and commonplace moments are just a means to forget our pain. But truly, these moments are sacred and beautiful. The moments of darkness that we spend with family and friends are the moments that we look back and see as pivotal to our healing and growth.

They are the stories we will share with others. They are the times we stretched and grew in our friendships and in our faith. God didn't put these people randomly into our lives. Our friends are the physical proof of God at work in our lives.

Some may balk at that. If you don't have friends that you are willing to allow into your life, it's not the friends who are at fault; and that is something I had to learn. I am a part of the male species of human; and we tend to have a far harder time building solid friendships than our better halves, our female counterparts.

I'm not going into why that is. That is for other people far smarter and wiser than I, but it tends to be true far more often than not.

## —So Men...

Let's lift some weights again.

Friends are hard to come by. What I really mean is brothers are hard to come by. When men get close, we become brothers. What is closer than a brother? At least, story-wise, brothers are the closest people. We look out for each other, we plot with each other, we climb mountains, we wade through valleys, and we back each other without question.

Brothers don't shy away from a storm. The jump in head first. Sometimes the wiser brother may even bring rain jackets.

You get my point. But the sad reality is that most men don't have brothers. We have football (I like football) friends. We have gaming friends. We have gym friends. We have drinking (water or gatorade, ladies, it's all good) friends. These are like part time friends, here for only parts of your life. But we don't have very many, if any, full time friends. We don't have friends who are not only willing to do battle for you, but often with you.

We call them brothers. Because in moments like these, when emotions are high, we need a brother that will barge his way in. Brothers couldn't care less about your manliness and will fight *for* you by fighting *against* your inane and asinine walls.

This time in your life might be the moment you find some. Sure, it's not a pull someone off the street corner and become brothers deal; but this is a time where you must open up. Not doing so will wreak havoc on your soul.

Don't destroy your own soul because you're manly.

# Where Are We Now?

Time doesn't heal. On the contrary, time can *mask* pain. It can do it so well that we think we have healed, but I can tell you that what is festering under that scar is not health or healing. It is not life.

I think that's where we get things wrong a lot. The passage of time diminishes the pain we feel so we begin to believe we are healing. After enough time, when we think of the painful situation, the pain doesn't slam us to the ground. So we're healed! Praise Jesus! . . . Right?

What's brewing inside you isn't the warmth of health and love but the heat of sepsis. It's a silent death that erodes at your emotions, your mental capacity. Soon, you're raging at people over not throwing away their used paper towel (I mean, they should be throwing it away). You get ticked off at your kids for not putting their plates in the sink.

You may not notice it, but others sure will. You are rapidly irritable, easily provoked, and constantly worn down. Life slowly (and usually unnoticeably) becomes a drag. This is true of any and all wounds that we let fester under scars. Some wounds bring it out faster. (The deeper the wound, the worse the sepsis will be if covered over by time).

We all know what I will say at this point: talk, scream, cry. The only way to get it out and truly begin to heal is getting before God and living in communion with people. Remember that people are often God's means of helping and answering prayers.

Friends, brothers and sisters, who are willing to wade through the valleys are the only way you will heal. There is no "sucking out the poison." It must run its course. And that is why we need each other. There will be times we simply can't carry on; we can't paddle. We need someone else to carry us. We need the faith of others to help heal us (Mark 2:1-12 - the faith of *the friends* is what carried the paralytic man to Jesus. *Their* faith is what brought healing to the man).

When we heal, and not just allow time to leave a scar, we find peace in our suffering, joy in our pain. We look back and see how people carried us when we were weak, how we kept moving in the darkness despite our desire to quit; and ultimately, we see the faithfulness of a God who has and does weep with us.

We find compassion from others and in ourselves.

We realize in these moments that, indeed, we weren't meant or created to be strong enough to shoulder all of life. We were meant to live together, to come alongside one another. We begin to see how God created us to be less about us and more about them. It's about bringing the light into darkness.

It's about the pain of never getting to hold my daughter but stepping up and carrying someone else through their struggle. It's about the horror of death but the exuberance of life found within Christ.

Yes, there is still sadness that I won't get to hold my only girl; but there is far more joy, peace, and love when I think of my Norah Kate.

* * *

If you are currently right in the midst of the loss of your child, I want to talk to you. This is a pain I truly believe no parent should ever have to know. I'm so sorry for your loss. I want to make it abundantly clear that this pain, this hollowness, this guilt, this sorrow will go away. Light *will* break the darkness.

But it sure doesn't feel like it at times.

Keep walking. Keep paddling. If you are married, please continue to be. Continue to seek each other. Men, seek out your wife. Women, seek out your husband. Both of you may not want to talk, but the silence that surrounds the two of you when you are holding each other will speak for you.

If you are not married, seek family—whoever that may be. Whether it is blood or by choice, seek them. Having people around is key to getting passed this.

When the pain is too great, cry out. If you need to, get in the car and drive somewhere. Scream and yell all you want. Let loose your pain, your anger, your sadness. In stillness release your pain to God.

He is big enough.

He is strong enough.

He is who we were created for and by.

He knows your pain.

He knows your sorrow.

He is crying with you.

He is longing for you.

These moments are terrible, but we can use them. Even in our pain we can learn to draw near to God. We can learn to take all the hate, all the pain, and cast our cares on him. His strength will sustain you. You can persevere, you can make it through this. (1 Peter 5:7, Matthew 11:28-30, Hebrews 12:1-2)

* * *

May you find peace in your suffering, grace in your pain, and strength in your weakness. May you run to our Father and welcome those He brings to you. May you find rest upon the shoulders of good men and women who are willing to lean into the darkness with you. And may you understand that God is big enough—that He created you and knows you and loves you and wants you and craves the best for you. May you run to Him, for he is on your side.

# Notes

# Notes

# Notes

# Notes

# Notes

# Notes

# About The Author

Life is filled with joys and horrors. A parent should never outlive their child, but sometimes that happens. After experiencing it first hand, ryan took to writing. He prays his story will be a light and a hope to you and to others who are or have been in the same situation. He's a firefighter and author/publisher. He lives in Texas with his wife and four boys.

For more from ryan, visit bkbkr.com or blackcoralpress.com.
Connect with him on Twitter or Instagram: **@thebookbaker**

# Norah Kate

Published by Black Coral Press. The black coral logo © copyright Black Coral Press. For information regarding permission, write to Black Coral Press at permissions@blackcoralpress.com.

We hope that this book has meant something to you. If you have suffered a miscarriage, know that you are being prayed for. Even though we (probably) don't know your name, you are being prayed for.

For more visit norahkate.com.

Also, please give this book to anyone that might benefit from this. This book is not about make the author rich, so we encourage you to give it away. Pay it forward by being someone else's rescue.

Paddle onward.

Print ISBN: 978-0-9969188-2-4
eBook ISBN: 978-0-9969188-3-1

First edition, August 2020
Book and cover design by ryan baker

www.ingramcontent.com/pod-product-compliance
Lightning Source LLC
Chambersburg PA
CBHW020521030426
42337CB00011B/500